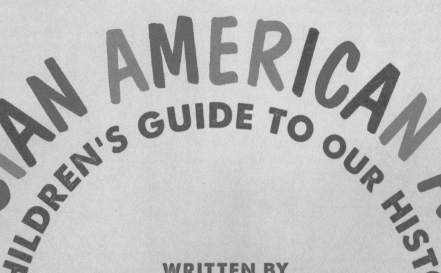

AN ASIAN AMERICAN A TO Z
A CHILDREN'S GUIDE TO OUR HISTORY

WRITTEN BY
CATHY LINH CHE
AND
KYLE LUCIA WU

ILLUSTRATED BY
KAVITA RAMCHANDRAN

Haymarket Books
Chicago, Illinois

For Kiên, my dimple twin—KLW

For Legend, Athenea, Pierce, and Ari—CLC

For my children K and V—KR

Published in 2023 by
Haymarket Books
P.O. Box 180165
Chicago, IL 60618
www.haymarketbooks.org
ISBN: 978-1-64259-945-9

Distributed to the trade through Consortium Book Sales and Distribution.

Printed in Canada

Library of Congress Cataloging-in-Publication data is available.

10 9 8 7 6 5 4 3 2 1

A is for **Asian American!** Many fought for you and a name for us all, collective and true.

For immigrants, refugees, workers, and students, to choose one name was the start of our movement.

B is for **beginning**. When did you start?
From where did you or your family depart?

In 1776, the US was formed.
Did you know Asians arrived years before?

How did you begin? Go ask your kin!
How did I become Asian American?

I HAVE A DREAM...

MARTIN LUTHER KING JR.

C

C is for **civil rights**. At the time,
    unfair rules
forced Black Americans into
    separate schools.

For equal treatment and protection
    from laws—
many marched and struggled
    for the cause.

Asian Americans everywhere
    owe much of our fight
to the brave ones who first stood up
    for civil rights.

3

D is for **demand**, to speak out, to shout,
to show up for others, to bring change about.

We gathered in airports, voices strong and clear:
No Muslim Bans ever! We want justice here!

E is for **exclusion**, to deny entry, shut out.
The Chinese were the first group to be locked out.

They were banned from the US for eighty-plus years,
for no reason besides our country's fear.

When the Exclusion Act ended, they migrated in waves.
In a country that had made laws against them, they had to be brave.

F

F is for being **first**, a leader of your times.
So many have been bold enough to walk a new line:

from Sunisa Lee, Olympic gold medalist,
to Rashida Tlaib, first Palestinian woman in Congress,

to Bruno Mars, whose diamond albums are the best,
to Padma Lakshmi, an author, model, and host of *Top Chef*,

to Kala Bagai and Bhagat Singh Thind,
who fought to become American citizens.

To you! What new lines would you like to chart?
You can walk a new path, one lit by your heart.

BRUNO MARS

PADMA LAKSHMI

SUNISA LEE

7

G is for **Grace Lee Boggs**, a feminist activist whose ideas were radically anticapitalist.

In her home of Detroit, she wanted youth to feel whole. Her community gardens gave them pride in their role.

The only way to survive is by taking care of one another, she said. Treat those around you like siblings, sisters, and brothers.

H is for **hotel**. I-Hotel is where seniors lived
until rich villains went in to evict!

Evict means to take someone's home away.
I-Hotel was the only place they could afford to stay.

So protesters stood, linked hand-in-hand.
They were kicked out, yet continued to stand.

Years later, a new I-Hotel was made!
Heroes don't give up if they don't win right away.

9

I is for **intersectionality**, how your selves overlap,
how gender, race, and class make up your own map.

It's for honoring all parts of someone,
respecting who they are, however they come.

J is for **Japanese American** incarceration.
During World War II, in this very nation,

120,000 were placed in incarceration camps in a blink.
Most were US citizens, which makes you think:

What does it mean to be a citizen here?
Don't we all deserve to be free without fear?

-STOP-
AREA LIMITS
FOR PERSONS OF
JAPANESE ANCESTRY
RESIDING IN THIS
RELOCATION CENTER

SENTRY
ON DUTY

K

K is for **kaleidoscope**—how many colors there are,
in Asian America, how many languages and stars:

South and Southeast, Central, East, and West,
Nepal and Laos, Kazakhstan, Taiwan, Bangladesh.

You belong if you're multiracial or an adoptee.
There isn't one kind of Asian American to be.

Though we joined together as a rallying call,
we'll never have one neat story for all.

Not every group is as visible, as seen.
Each has its own stories, differences, and dreams.

L is for **labor**, which first brought us here
on ships to plantations in the early years.

In California, bosses refused to pay workers fairly
for picking grapes in the blazing heat daily,

until Larry, César, and Dolores joined hands.
Filipinos and Mexicans became part of one band.

Black and Arab autoworkers chanted, *Free Palestine!*
showing we're more powerful together, time after time.

Let's stand with all workers calling out *STRIKE!*
United in victory, unity is our might.

LARRY ITLIONG

SUPPORT
FARM WORKERS

DON'T BE
UNFAIR
TO FARM
WORKERS

SIN MA
NO HA
FRITO

DELANO GRAPE STRIKERS
BOYCOTT GRAPES
ANOC - AWL CIO

HUELGA

DOLORES HUERTA

CÉSAR CHAVEZ

NEW YORK TAXI WORKERS ALLIANCE
RIGHTS. RESPECT. DIGNIT

STRIKE

LABOR RIGHTS

FREE PALESTINE

RS

use I am
TH it!

15

M is for **movies** on the silver screen—
growing up, Anna May Wong's biggest dream!

She starred in the first color film in 1923.
She did silent and sound films, on stage and TV.

Martial arts movies were shaped by Bruce Lee,
The Legend of the Ten Rings brought us Shang-Chi.

Kelly Marie Tran was Raya, warrior princess of Heart,
and Rose, a Star Wars pilot, brave and smart.

Comedians Hari, Hasan, and Ali make us laugh!
Directors Lulu and Mira create worlds with their craft.

Are there any parts that you want to play?
Your name could be up there in lights one day.

MIRA NAIR

HASAN MINHAJ

N is for **neighborhoods**, where we settle to sleep,
to be safe with our families, to work, live, and eat.

At first we weren't welcome in places we landed;
so we made our own havens to give each other a hand in.

We made Little Pakistan and Cambodia Town,
Little Uzbekistan, Tehrangeles, and Koreatown.

Always remember these neighborhoods grew,
to keep cultures and communities strong just for you.

19

O is for **oceans**, which our families crossed
by boat or by plane—oh, so much was lost!

From homelands changed by conflict and war,
we built new lives on this other shore.

P is for **Protect Mauna Kea**, tallest mountain on Earth,
a sacred place in Hawai'i we should respect and not hurt.

Asian Americans, offer your voices and hands
to join Pacific Islanders in their fair demands.

Decolonize Oceania! Free Guåhan!
For climate justice now, we march on.

Q is for **questions**, which you may be asked,
about where you're from, or your parents, or past.

But you don't have to answer! It's fine not to say!
You belong, and you never need to explain.

R

R is for **railroad**. For the first time in the US,
the Transcontinental Railroad linked East to West.

The work was hard, and the weather rough,
but the Chinese workers who helped build it were tough.

Without those men, we couldn't take those trains,
but history books left out all their names!

Next time you ride a train, think of what they've done.
We reclaim history by remembering each one.

S is for **soups**, how they slurp, how they soothe.
There are so many kinds that you can choose:

congee, aush, tom yum, laksa, and phở,
soondubu and chakna. With soup comes love!

T is for **Twin Towers**, which fell one September.
9/11 is a day the world will always remember.

I love New York more than ever was the city's one song,
yet many New Yorkers were treated like they didn't belong—

bullied and jailed like the Japanese before.
Then President Bush started two wars,

targeted our friends in Afghanistan and Iraq,
who were, for many years, under US attack.

The war created a new wave of refugees,
searching for safety, wanting to be free.

How do we decide who we welcome and protect?
Your words and your actions all have an effect.

U is for **university**, a school for higher education,
where we go to study and share information.

At schools like these, the Third World Liberation Front began.
Many groups came together with one list of demands.

They wanted to take classes that included their voices,
and called for Ethnic Studies to give them these choices.

They spoke truth to power and held strikes so long
the schools had to admit that they had been wrong.

In 1969, they won the battle at their schools!
When we fight for justice, we make our own rules.

V is for **Vincent Chin**. We honor his name.
We remember his story, though it's full of pain.

He was just twenty-seven in June '82,
when two white men attacked him because of his hue.

His death sparked outrage, protest, and sorrow.
Asian Americans worked together for a better tomorrow.

W is for **writers**. We have so many!
Authors who talk about our lives aplenty.

At Angel Island, many carved poems into walls.
Their private stories became messages to all.

Early on we had *Gidra* and *Bridge* magazines,
and Basement Workshop, a home of the arts scene.

Say it at the top of your lungs: *Aiiieeeee!*
That was the name of our first anthology.

Maxine Hong Kingston wrote a story of Mulan.
Long live Meena Alexander! Long live Etel Adnan!

Ocean Vuong said: *Prepare to be unfathomable.*
You, dear reader, can be anything imaginable.

X is for **expansive**, which
    means always growing.
There is simply no way of
    ever knowing

how the future will shape our
    family tree,
how Asian America will look or
    what it will be.

32

Y is for **Yuri Kochiyama**, a civil rights leader
   in Harlem, New York,
who befriended Malcolm X and joined in his work.

She spent her youth in an incarceration camp,
yet made service and activism her life stamp.

Tomorrow's world is yours to build, she said.
Take a moment and let those words fill your head.

Z is for **zoom**! Up, up, and away!
With all that you know, you can go any place.

There's power in knowing Asian American history:
who came before us, who helped us get free.

Now what will you do with all that you know?
The world is here waiting, watching you grow.

GLOSSARY

A is for Asian American

Asian American is a name we picked for ourselves! In 1968, **Yuji Ichioka** and **Emma Gee**, founders of the student group Asian American Political Alliance, chose the term "Asian American" to unite all Asians under one name. Some of us are **immigrants**, people who arrived from a different country. Others, **refugees**, are people who left their home countries because they were not safe. Though each group had different experiences, the students knew that joining together under one shared name gave them strength.

B is for Beginning

Before America's **beginning**, Filipino fishermen lived as a community in Louisiana in 1763. They jumped from Spanish ships to escape work as indentured servants on plantations. Indentured servants work without pay for travel, food, and housing. Sometimes, they worked their whole lives and were never freed.

C is for Civil Rights

During the 1950s, '60s, and '70s, Black Americans fought for their **civil rights**. They couldn't attend the same schools, use the same bathrooms, or drink from the same water fountains as white Americans. Leaders like **Martin Luther King Jr.**, **Malcolm X**, and **Rosa Parks** helped change these unfair laws. The Asian American Movement started in solidarity with that justice movement, and Asians immigrating to the United States all benefited from the advances made from the civil rights movement.

D is for Demand

In 2017, thousands of protesters in airports **demanded** to stop rules that discriminated against people because of their religion. Former president Donald Trump tried to keep people from entering the US. The Muslim Ban was unfair and separated many people from their families.

E is for Exclusion

The Chinese **Exclusion** Act of 1882 was the first law to prevent an ethnic group from entering the country. Others were passed in 1892, 1902, and 1924. Exclusion acts were in place until the Immigration Act of 1965 when the rules were changed, and Chinese and other Asian immigrants were allowed to enter the United States.

F is for First

Sunisa Lee is the first Hmong American to win an Olympic gold for women's gymnastics. **Rashida Tlaib** is the first Palestinian American woman elected to Congress. **Bruno Mars** is the first musician to have five diamond songs in the US. **Padma Lakshmi** is the first Indian model to have a career in Paris, Milan, and New York. **Kala Bagai** became one of the first South Asian women on the West Coast. In 2020, a street in Berkeley was named after her! **Bhagat Singh Thind** won citizenship after a battle with the Supreme Court, which stated that only white Americans could become citizens.

G is for Grace Lee Boggs

Grace Lee Boggs's values light up the way. She was an important figure in Detroit's Black Power movement, the Detroit Asian Political Alliance, and anti-Vietnam War protests. She was a **feminist** (someone who believes women should have equal rights, opportunities, and power), **activist** (a person who works to create social change), and **anticapitalist** (someone who believes we should share what we have with others). The Boggs Center taught young people to create beautiful gardens in Detroit.

H is for Hotel

I-**Hotel**, or International Hotel, in San Francisco, California, has an important place in Asian American history. Older Filipino and Chinese men lived there. In 1968, there was a plan to push out these elders, but activists worked to keep them in their homes.

I is for Intersectionality

Intersectionality is the word that **Kimberlé Crenshaw** created to describe the ways that many parts come together to form who we are: our race, class, and gender. Your race might be described as Asian, Black, Latinx, Arab, or Indigenous. Class is connected to how much money your family has. Gender might be boy, girl, trans, or nonbinary. All of these together make up who we are!

J is for Japanese American Incarceration

After Pearl Harbor in Hawai'i was attacked, President Franklin Delano Roosevelt sent Japanese Americans to incarceration camps. Most were American citizens, but the US said they looked like the enemy. They lived in incarceration camps in California, Arizona, Wyoming, Utah, Arkansas, and Colorado.

K is for Kaleidoscope

Kaleidoscopes have many colors, patterns, and shapes. Similarly, Asian Americans also vary by ethnicities, languages, and histories.

L is for Labor

Labor means work. The first Asian Americans came to the United States and labored on plantations and on railroads for low pay. They organized labor strikes so bosses would pay them better. In Delano, California, **Larry Itliong**, **Dolores Huerta**, and **César Chávez** formed the United Farm Workers and went on strike for years until they won.

M is for Movies

Anna May Wong was the first Chinese American movie star. Born in Los Angeles's Chinatown, she was in sixty films! Wong and **Bruce Lee** paved the way for many more: **Kelly Marie Tran** won fame in *Star Wars* and then played in *Raya and the Last Dragon*. **Hari Kondabolu**, **Hasan Minhaj**, and **Ali Wong** are comedians, and **Lulu Wang** and **Mira Nair** have directed their own movies.

N is for Neighborhoods

Asian immigrants created **neighborhoods** full of their own customs, foods, and communities. **Cambodia Town** is on the east side of Long Beach, California, and **Tehrangeles** is in Los

Angeles and Orange County! You can find **Little Pakistan** on Coney Island in Brooklyn or go to **Little Uzbekistan**. There are **Koreatowns** throughout the US.

O is for Oceans

Many Asian Americans traveled over **oceans** to begin new lives in the US. After the fall of Saigon, in 1975, refugees came to the US from Vietnam, Cambodia, and Laos. Today, refugees from Afghanistan, Iraq, and more are arriving. Our community is filled with those who rebuild life and family in a new land!

P is for Protect Mauna Kea

Native Hawaiians need our help to preserve and **protect** their sacred land, including the holy **Mauna Kea**, a dormant volcano on Hawai'i's Big Island that the US government wants to build a telescope on top of. Join the chants: **Decolonize Oceania!** (Australasia, Melanesia, Micronesia, and Polynesia) and **Free Guåhan!** (the indigenous name for Guam).

Q is for Questions

The **questions**: Where are you from? Or where are you really from? can make Asian Americans feel foreign in our own country. These questions are microaggressions, or everyday acts of racism that often go unnoticed. Remember: You don't have to answer any questions you don't want to!

R is for Railroad

The **Transcontinental Railroad** made train travel across the entire United States possible. It made isolated parts of the country easier to get to. The nearly 20,000 Chinese workers had the hardest, most dangerous jobs. Still they earned half wages, worked six days a week, and had to buy their own food! In a famous photo from May 1869, workers toast champagne to celebrate the rail's completion—but no Chinese workers are in the photo.

S is for Soups

Soups exist in every culture! **Congee** is the Chinese name for rice porridge, called **jūk** in Korean. More styles of rice porridge include **cháo** in Vietnam, **hsan pyok** in Burma, **bâbâr** in Cambodia, **arroz caldo** in the Philippines, and **okayu** in Japan. In Iranian and Afghan cuisine, **aush** or **ash** is a thick noodle soup with chickpeas, beans, meat, and yogurt. **Tom yum goong** is a sour Thai soup with lemongrass, galangal, kaffir lime leaves, and bird's eye chilies. **Laksa** is a spicy Malaysian, Indonesian, and Singaporean noodle soup with noodles and curry. **Chakna** is a spicy Indian stew with goat tripe. **Soondubu** is a Korean spicy soft tofu stew. **Phở** is a Vietnamese soup with rice noodles, herbs, and slices of beef.

T is for Twin Towers

The **Twin Towers** were once the tallest buildings in the world. On September 11, 2001, two airplanes crashed into them, killing nearly 3,000 people. The attacks made some Americans feel patriotic. The attacks also created a terrible wave of anti-Muslim sentiment. In 2002, the US forced people from countries with a lot of Muslims to register with the government. Many people who followed the new rule were set to be deported.

U is for University

In the 1960s the **Universities** San Francisco State and UC Berkeley were where the **Third World Liberation Front**, a multiracial coalition, began. Black, Asian, and Latinx students joined together, calling on their universities to provide fair education about their cultures and address existing racism. These student strikes were met with resistance and violence, but the students prevailed, winning ethnic studies departments for their universities!

V is for Vincent Chin

Vincent Chin was celebrating with friends when Ronald Ebens and Michael Nitz, two white men who worked in the car industry, saw him. Back then, the Japanese car industry was thriving, leading many Americans to unfairly discriminate against anyone who looked Asian. Ebens and Nitz argued with Vincent and tragically beat him to death, but they didn't face any consequences for doing so. Vincent's death outraged the Asian American community, who protested his unfair death.

W is for Writers

Asian American **writers** have a long history! Thousands of Chinese immigrants held at **Angel Island** carved poems into the walls of their rooms, leaving stories of how it felt to be held in a cell when they got to America, the land of freedom and dreams. Other writers are in the Los Angeles-based *Gidra*, "the voice of the Asian American experience." *Bridge: The Magazine of Asians in America* started in 1971 at the Basement Workshop, an Asian American arts collective in Chinatown, New York City, in the 1970s and '80s. *Aiiieeeee!* was the first book in the US to include Chinese, Japanese, and Filipino American writers. **Maxine Hong Kingston** retold the Chinese folktale of Fa Mu Lan in her book, *The Woman Warrior*. **Meena Alexander** explored migration, feminism, and memory. **Etel Adnan** was a Lebanese American poet, essayist, and painter. **Ocean Vuong** is a Vietnamese American poet and writer raised in Hartford, Connecticut.

X is for Expansive

Asian American identity is **expansive** and expanding. We continue to welcome new kinds of Asian Americans with each passing year.

Y is for Yuri Kochiyama

Yuri Kochiyama was a Japanese American political activist born in California. Yuri spent two years in an Arkansas incarceration camp with her family. As an adult in New York, she fought for civil and human rights, Black liberation, against the war in Vietnam, and to free all political prisoners. She and her husband also worked to get the US to admit the damage it did to Japanese Americans.

Z is for Zoom

Zoom to great heights with all you know. When our history is left out of schools, it's even more important for us to learn our legacy. What you know is your power. Let it help you shape our world.

Acknowledgments

Grateful acknowledgement to Summer Farah, Swati Khurana, Sarah Park Dahlen, and Craig Santos Perez, who looked at earlier versions of this manuscript and helped us shape it into a more inclusive children's book. With love to the Asian American communities that have shaped us and helped us grow, and to Kundiman, which is forever.

About the Authors

Cathy Linh Che is a Vietnamese American writer who grew up in Los Angeles and is now based in New York City. She is the author of the poetry book *Split* (Alice James Books), winner of the Kundiman Poetry Prize, the Norma Farber First Book Award from the Poetry Society of America, and the Best Poetry Book Award from the Association of Asian American Studies. She works as executive director at Kundiman, and her website is cathylinhche.com.

Kyle Lucia Wu grew up in a small town in New Jersey and is now a writer based in Brooklyn, New York. She is the author of *Win Me Something* (Tin House Books), an NPR Best Book of the Year, and was an Asian American Writers' Workshop Margins Fellow. Her work has been published in *Literary Hub*, *Catapult*, *BOMB Magazine*, and *Guernica*. She works as the deputy director at Kundiman, and her website is kyleluciawu.com.

About the Illustrator

Kavita Ramchandran is an illustrator and graphic designer based in New York City, though she is originally from Mumbai, India. She has art directed and illustrated for children's magazines and apps, designed elementary school textbooks, and created the animated shorts *Maya the Indian Princess* and *Happy Holi, Maya!* for Nick Jr. Her first picture book, *Dancing in Thatha's Footsteps*, written by Srividhya Venkat, won the 2022 South Asia Book Award. Her website is wemakebelieve.com